To Leona, Romy, Maggie, Matilda, Niall,
Annabelle, Ellerie, and Adrian
A. B.

To Grace and Milo, with all my love—
may you always know God's greatest love
E. S.

"*C is for Christian* is both a tool and a treasure for anyone—child or adult—who wants to follow Christ. Alistair Begg's clear teaching and insightful questions help readers respond personally to God's truth, bringing theology within the reach of young and old alike. I strongly recommend this beautiful book for every home library."

Jani Ortlund, Renewal Ministries; Author, *Help! I'm Married to My Pastor*

"When children think about the marks of a Christian, they may first think of things Christians do. But it's also essential for us to teach kids who Christians *are*. That's exactly what Dr. Begg does in *C Is for Christian*. This beautifully illustrated alphabet catechism will help the next generation learn and remember the Bible's many vivid depictions of Christian identity."

Jared Kennedy, Editor, The Gospel Coalition; Author, *The Beginner's Gospel Story Bible*

"As a grandfather, I am always on the hunt for gospel-rich books to read to my grandchildren. *C is for Christian* is a book I'll be reading to my grandkids. With simple everyday-life illustrations to help children comprehend big ideas, Alistair Begg explains what it means to be a Christian. Every family will want to add this book to their library."

Marty Machowski, Family Pastor; Author, *The Ology, WonderFull*, and *The Treasure*

"*C is for Christian* is a remarkable resource. It beautifully simplifies the essence of our faith into bite-sized, digestible pieces that resonate well with young hearts. The combination of captivating illustrations, thoughtful questions, and prayers in each segment not only delights young readers visually but also stirs their curiosity and fosters impactful family conversations about God's love and faith's blessings. It's a perfect resource for parents looking to lay a solid spiritual foundation in their children's hearts."

Portia Collins, Bible Teacher; Host, *Grounded* podcast at Revive Our Hearts; Founder, She Shall Be Called

Alistair Begg

C is for

Christian

An A to Z Treasury of Who We Are in Christ

ILLUSTRATED BY Emma Skerratt

C is for Christian
© Alistair Begg, 2024

Published by:
The Good Book Company

thegoodbook.com | thegoodbook.co.uk
thegoodbook.com.au | thegoodbook.co.nz | thegoodbook.co.in

Published in association with the literary agency of Wolgemuth & Wilson.

Illustration by Emma Skerratt | Art direction and design by André Parker

ISBN: 9781802541069 | JOB-007617 | Printed in India

What words would you use to describe what a squirrel is and what a squirrel is like?

What words would you use to tell me about your best friend?

I imagine you used quite a few different words to answer those questions. No one word can sum up what a squirrel is like. No single word can describe your best friend to me. The words "squirrel" and "best friend" need a whole list of other words to explain them.

It's the same with the word "Christian." Being a Christian is the most wonderful, exciting, life-changing thing anyone can be. But... what is a Christian? What words can we use to describe what it means to call yourself a Christian?

In this book, you'll find 26 words that complete this sentence: A Christian is...

To help you remember them, they each start with a different letter of the alphabet. Think of this as an A to Z of what a Christian is. As you'll discover, there's even one for "C" that isn't "Christian"! You can read through this book in any order, but I imagine most people will start at A and work through to Z, and then return to their favorites...

I hope you enjoy your time in this book. I hope that, as you read, you'll become more and more amazed by all that God has done and is doing for His people—for every Christian, however young or old. And I pray that you'll want to become, or continue to be, a Christian yourself.

With love,

Adopted

"You have received the Spirit of adoption as sons,
by whom we cry, 'Abba, Father!'"

Romans 8:15

When someone is adopted, what happens to them?

Here's a happy story about a boy finding a new family. Imagine this boy is called Simeon. He is an orphan—he doesn't have parents. He lives in an orphanage. He doesn't have a home of his own or a family of his own. He has very few clothes and hardly any toys.

Then imagine that one day, a kind man called Mr. Billingsgate visits the orphanage. He sees Simeon, and he chooses to love him. He makes Simeon a member of his family—to live in his house and get his own clothes and toys. Simeon gets to be called "Simeon Billingsgate" to show he's joined this new family, and he gets to call Mr. Billingsgate "Father."

Simeon has been adopted.

You might know some children who have been adopted. You might have been adopted yourself. If so, your parents chose to make you part of their family, to love you, and to share what they have with you.

One of the ways the Bible describes people who trust in Jesus as their King and Savior is "adopted." God is kind, and He chooses to love us and make us a member of His family—to make us His son or daughter. He gives us what we need. One day, we will live in His house in heaven. We have countless brothers and sisters—everyone else who trusts Jesus is part of this family. Best of all, we get to call God "Father" and know that He is always loving us and looking after us.

Now, imagine that Simeon has settled happily into his new family. What might he want to say to Mr. Billingsgate? I guess he might want to say, "Thank you"!

And how might Simeon feel about being in his new family? I guess he'd feel joyful and loved.

If you trust Jesus, God has adopted you into His wonderful family. Wow! You'll want to say, "Thank you." And you can feel joyful and loved.

 is for Adopted.

What is great about being adopted by God?

Is there something you feel sad or worried about? What difference will it make to remember that, if you love Jesus, God has adopted you?

Dear Father, thank You that anyone who trusts in Jesus is Your adopted child, and can call You Father. Thank You that You are kind and generous. Thank You that You love and look after all Your children, all the time. Please keep me trusting Jesus, and please keep reminding me how great it is to be Your adopted child. Amen.

Branch

"I am the vine; you are the branches."

John 15:5

What happens to a branch if it is chopped off its tree?

Vines are plants with lots of branches. And grapes grow on the branches. In this verse, Jesus is saying that anyone who loves and trusts in Him is joined to Him like a branch is joined to a vine.

When a branch is joined to a vine, all the goodness in the vine flows to the branch. That's what makes the branches alive. When we love Jesus, all of His goodness—His life and His power—flows into us, and we enjoy life with him now and forever.

You can tell a branch is joined to a vine by the fruit it grows. These branches don't grow apples, because they're not part of an apple tree. They don't grow avocados, because they're not part of an avocado tree. They grow grapes, because they're part of a grapevine!

People who trust Jesus grow fruit too. Not apples or avocados or grapes. They grow the fruit of being like Jesus—loving, joyful, peaceful, patient, kind, good, loyal, gentle, and self-controlled.

So Christians are branches. We stay connected to Jesus, the vine, by loving and trusting Him. And then we have life forever, and we grow more and more like Jesus.

 is for Branch.

What is good about being a branch with Jesus as our vine?

Can you think of "fruit" that Jesus is growing in you because you are His branch, loving and trusting Him?

Dear Lord Jesus, thank You that we can be connected to You like a branch, just by loving and trusting in You. Thank You that You give us life. Thank You that You grow fruit in us by Your Spirit. Please work in us so we become more and more like You. Amen.

Citizen

"Our citizenship is in heaven."

Philippians 3:20

Which country are you a citizen of?

Everyone is a citizen of a country. It's the place where they most belong. If they have a passport, it's the country that gave them that passport. And they speak like and behave like people from that country speak and behave.

So if you are an American citizen, then you belong to America, and you speak like an American and behave like an American—even if you travel outside America, you are still an American citizen. If you are French, then you belong to France, and you speak French and behave like a French person—even if you travel outside France, you are still a French citizen.

Christians are citizens of heaven. This means the place where we most belong is not here, where we live at the moment. It's heaven, with Jesus. So this also means that the place where we will be most happy living is not here but heaven, with Jesus. At the moment we do not live in heaven—we are in this world. But if we are followers of Jesus, we are citizens of heaven. Yes, we are still American or French or British or Brazilian citizens... but most important of all, we are citizens of heaven.

This will make a difference to how we speak and how we behave. We will speak kind words like Jesus, and we will act like Jesus. This will also make a difference to how we think about this world. This world is not our real home. Heaven is—and heaven is much better than anything here. That's where we belong, and that's where we are heading. How exciting!

 is for Citizen.

Can you think of things that are better about heaven than this world?

Where is a Christian's real home? How does that make you feel?

Dear Lord Jesus, thank You that You have given us a home in heaven, where everything is perfect and we can live with You. Please help us to remember that we belong there, not in this world. Please make us excited about living with You as citizens of heaven forever. Amen.

Dwelled-in

"That Christ may dwell in your hearts
through faith."
Ephesians 3:17

What things in your house show that your family lives there?

Imagine walking past a house every week. It's broken down. There are weeds growing up its walls. The curtains are hanging off their poles, and some of the windows are broken.

Then one day, as you walk past, you notice a huge difference. The weeds have been cleared. The windows have been replaced, and there are new curtains. It looks new and welcoming.

What has happened? The house has a new owner, who has been working to make this house their home. How wonderful for that house to have an owner who cares for it!

A Christian is a person in whose heart Jesus lives. Yes, He dwells in heaven—but, by His Spirit, He also dwells in His people. If you have faith in Jesus, then His home address is... your heart! He's not just a guest, like someone staying for a week and then going to live somewhere else. He's moved in to stay. That means that wherever you go, Jesus is with you. Wherever you are, you are not alone.

Having Jesus living in us makes a huge difference. Jesus changes people He dwells in. We see this in what happened to Zacchaeus, the little man who climbed a tree because he wanted to see Jesus passing through his town (Luke 19:1-10). When Jesus reached the tree, He told Zacchaeus that He was going to stay in Zacchaeus' house. And this changed Zacchaeus. Before, he had loved money. He had stolen and cheated to get more money. Now that Jesus was in his house, he loved Jesus. So he wanted to give his money away to help and care for others.

When Jesus dwells in someone, He works in them through His Spirit to make them more and more like Him. They become more kind, generous, joyful, and thoughtful. How wonderful to have Jesus dwelling in us, caring for us and changing us!

 is for Dwelled-in.

Where in this world does Jesus live?

Can you think of ways Jesus is changing you to make you more like him?

Dear Lord Jesus, thank You that You dwell in Your people, by Your Spirit. I would like to invite You to live in me. Please make me a person who is more and more a good home for You to live in. Please care for me and change me. Amen.

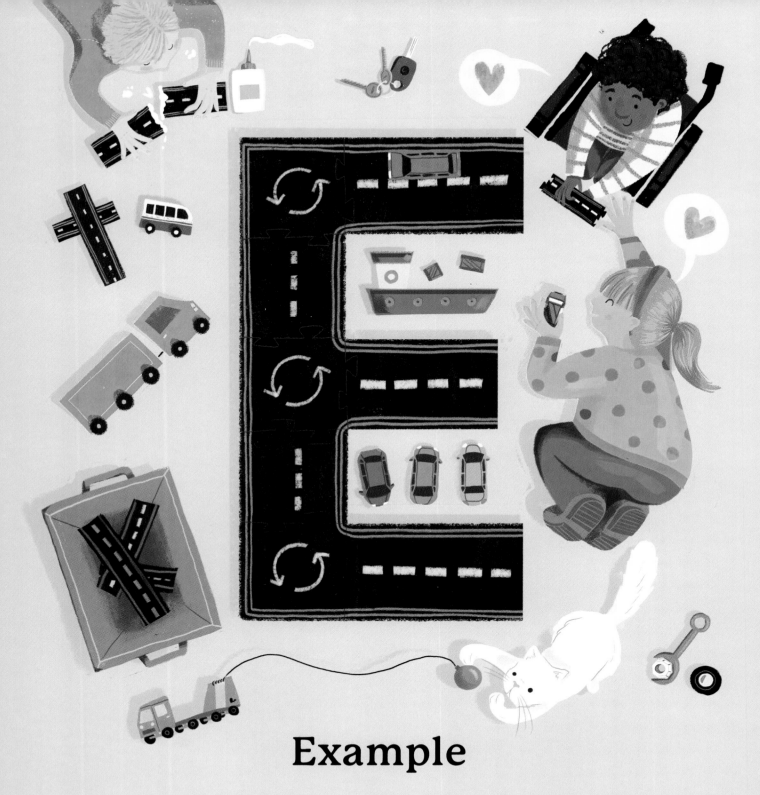

Example

"Let no one despise you for your youth, but set the believers
an example in speech, in conduct, in love, in faith, in purity."
1 Timothy 4:12

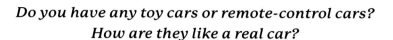

Do you have any toy cars or remote-control cars?
How are they like a real car?

An example is something that shows you what something else is like. When you look at a toy car, you can see what a real car is like—it has the same shape, and it has wheels, and it moves.

A Christian is someone who can help other people see what Jesus is like. They set an example that shows others what Jesus is like. And anyone can do this, even people who are youthful—even young children, like you.

Our verse gives us five ways we can set an example that shows people what Jesus is like:

1. By the way that you *speak*. When you say things that are kind and true and helpful, you are showing what Jesus is like.
2. By your *conduct*—which means by the way you behave. When you act in ways that obey God, you are showing what Jesus is like.
3. By your *love*. When you love people who have been unkind to you, you are showing what Jesus is like.
4. By your *faith*. When you trust God to be in charge of your life, and when you pray because you know He is in charge and you trust Him, you are showing what Jesus is like.
5. By your *purity*—which means by avoiding sin. When you say no to doing something that is wrong, you are showing what Jesus is like.

It is not easy to live as an example of what Jesus is like! So Jesus gives us His Holy Spirit to help us live in this way.

 is for Example.

How old do you need to be to set an example of what Jesus is like?

How can you be a good example of what Jesus is like in your day today?

Dear Lord Jesus, thank You that I can show other people what You are like. I don't always find this easy, so please work in me by Your Spirit so that I will become more like You in what I say, what I do, how I love people, how I trust God, and how I say no to what is wrong. Amen.

Forgiven

"Blessed is the one whose transgression is forgiven,
whose sin is covered."

Psalm 32:1

When you know you've done something wrong, how do you feel?
What do you do about it?

Imagine you are wearing a brand new, clean white top, and your mom tells you not to get anything on it. But you decide to play with paint, and you get some down the front.

You try to wipe it off. But paint stains.

You try to hide it. But it's all down the front.

You wonder if maybe your mom will only notice the clean parts of the top. But the paint is still there, on the front.

You can't clean your top, and you can't hide the stain. What you need is a new top—but you don't have one.

But then your brother or sister comes in. They offer to take your dirty top and give you their clean one.

Wow!

Our sin—the ways we don't love God and don't live with him as our King—is like a stain. We can't wipe it away—it is still there. We can't hide it—it is still there. Even the good things we have done can't cover it up. Who can help us?

Jesus can.

On the cross, Jesus took our sins, or transgressions, onto Himself. (That is, He took the sins of everyone who asks Him for forgiveness.) And He gave us His own totally clean perfection instead. It's as if He took our stained top and gave us His clean one. Jesus was punished instead of us. And we are forgiven!

Wow!

This is why the "one whose transgression is forgiven" is "blessed." Blessed means very happy. Our sin has been taken by Jesus and forgiven by God. We don't need to try to hide it or make up for it. We're forgiven. What a happy way to live!

 is for Forgiven.

What is wonderful about knowing that when we ask God to forgive us, He will?

Think about what Jesus did so that you can be forgiven. How does that make you feel? What does it make you want to say to Jesus?

Dear Father, thank You that I don't need to try to clean up my sin, or hide it, or make up for it. Thank You that You are always ready to forgive me when I am truly sorry. Thank You, Lord Jesus, that You died so that I can be forgiven and can enjoy life with You forever. Amen.

Giver

"God loves a cheerful giver."

2 Corinthians 9:7

How do you feel when someone gives you something good?
How do you feel when you share something good?

I have two sisters. When I was a child, sometimes we would go on long car journeys. Sometimes, one of my sisters would have some sweets for the journey.

If it was one of my sisters (we'll call her Gertie), when I said, "Please can you give me one of your sweets?" she'd say, "No—they're mine!" But if it was the other sister (we'll call her Kathy), when I asked her to give me a sweet, she'd usually say, "Yes, I'll give you a sweet. You can have two! Here you go."

Kathy was a giver. She was happy to give me things.

Christians are givers. We are called to give to God.

If you have money, you can give some of it to God. You can give God praise. You can give Him thanks. You can give Him your obedience.

Did you spot in our verse that God loves it when we give to Him in a particular way? God loves a cheerful giver. He doesn't love it if we give Him these things because we think we *have* to. He loves it when we give because we *want* to.

Most of the time, most of us like to get things more than we like to give things. So we need to remember that everything we have is a gift from God. When we give something to Him, we're only giving Him back what He's given us. And God will keep on giving us everything we need. When we remember that God will give us all we need and that everything we have is a gift from Him, then we will give Him all we can, and we will do it cheerfully.

We can enjoy giving to God. And we can know that God loves it when we do.

 is for Giver.

What would you like to give to God?

Can you think of things that God has given you? How does that make you feel?

Dear God, thank You for giving me eternal life by sending Jesus to take my sin. Thank You that every day You give me everything You know I need. Please show me what I can give to You, and how I can give to others around me. Please keep reminding me how much You have given me, so that I can give cheerfully to You and to others. Amen.

Helper

"Encourage the fainthearted, help
the weak, be patient."
1 Thessalonians 5:14

Who is the most helpful person in your class or in your family?
What things to do they do to help?

E very day, in lots and lots of ways, you can be helpful.
You can help your mom and dad in the house by doing the dishes, or setting the table, or cleaning your room. (I'm sure you can think of other ways as well!)

You can help a friend who is upset by being kind to them, or making a card for them, or giving them a present.

You can help at church by smiling at people around you, or thanking the people who teach you from the Bible, or offering to help clear things away afterwards.

The Bible tells us that God is a Helper (Psalm 54:4). Jesus came and helped us by dying so that we can be forgiven. And God sent the Holy Spirit to His people to be our Helper (John 14:26). When you help, you are being like God.

God does not just say He helps us. He actually does it! Being a helper is not just about calling yourself helpful. It is about being helpful. I could walk around wearing a baseball cap that said "Helper" on it. That wouldn't make me a helper. The key is in our actions—what we do.

This week, you can be like God and show people that you belong to Jesus by being helpful.

 is for Helper.

Why is it easier to say you'll be helpful than to actually be helpful?

Can you think of two or three new ways you can be helpful to others?

Dear God, we praise You that You are the greatest helper. Thank You, Jesus, that You died so that we can be forgiven. Thank You, Holy Spirit, that You help us live God's way each day. Thank You that I can show others what You are like by being a helper. Please show me ways that You would like me be helpful today. Amen.

Imitator

"Be imitators of God, as beloved children."
Ephesians 5:1

How good are you at copying what someone else does?

Sometimes children decide to imitate everything that one of their friends says or one of their parents says. It's very funny, as long as you don't do it for too long!

Children are usually good at closely following someone else's example. You watch how someone else cleans their teeth, and you learn how to do it. You watch how someone spells a word, and you learn how to do it. You watch how someone mows the grass, and you learn how to do it.

Christians are called to imitate God. We don't do this to become His children. We do it because we already are His children, if we are trusting Jesus as our Lord and Savior. We are to copy God!

How do we do that? Well, God came to earth as a man, and so, as we follow the example of Jesus Christ, we are imitating God. And Ephesians 5:2 tells us to "walk in love, as Christ loved us."

When we think, we should make sure we are loving others in how we think of them.

When we speak, we should make sure we are loving others in how we talk about them.

When we act, we should make sure we are loving others in what we do for them.

That's how Jesus loves us. He always loves us, no matter what. He loves us so much that He was willing to die for us. How amazing! And because we admire Jesus, we want to imitate Him.

You can love like Jesus in how you think of people and how you speak to people and what you do for people.

That's how you copy God. Imitate Jesus, and you will not go wrong.

I is for Imitator.

Can you think of some ways Jesus shows His love for you? What does that make you want to say to Him?

Think of one particular way that you can show Jesus' love to a particular person this week.

Dear Lord Jesus, thank You that You are God the Son and that You show me what God is like. Thank You that You always love me, all the time. Please make me better and better at imitating You so that I am able to love others in a way that pleases You. Make me quick to see ways I can copy You. Amen.

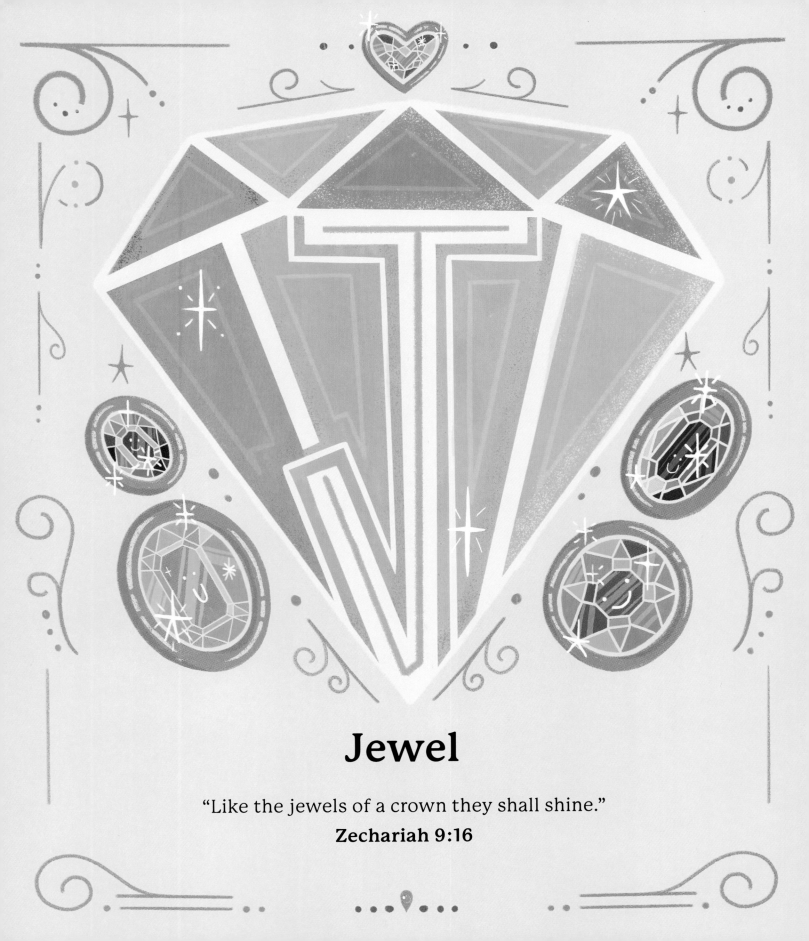

Jewel

"Like the jewels of a crown they shall shine."

Zechariah 9:16

Why do people put on jewelry?

When someone wears jewelry, the idea is not to get people to look at the jewels themselves. The idea is that as they sparkle, they help people see the beauty of the person who is wearing them.

God says that He has jewels that shine and show how amazing He is. But those jewels aren't diamonds or sapphires or emeralds or amethysts. No—they are His people! Boys and girls who trust Christ as their Savior are jewels in His crown. When we love Him and live His way, we are showing people how great He is. We are sparkling like jewels!

Jewels often sparkle best when they are part of a piece of jewelry. The jeweler has decided just how to arrange them so that each jewel sparkles as much as possible. That's what God has done with His jewels too. He decides where He wants us. He decides where we'll live, and where we'll go each day, and who we'll meet and be friends with. Those are the places where He wants us to sparkle, showing how great He is.

And God has all sizes and shapes of jewels. You might only be little, but sometimes the most beautiful jewels are the smallest ones. You might only be little, but you can sparkle brightly!

If you are a child who trusts Jesus as your King and your Savior, then you are a jewel in God's crown. Whether you're big or little, wherever you are you can sparkle by loving God and living His way, and then you will show people how great God is.

 is for Jewel.

Why is it exciting to be one of God's jewels?

Where will you go tomorrow? How can you sparkle as one of God's jewels while you are there?

Dear God, thank You for bringing me into Your people. Thank You that I can show people how great Jesus is. Thank You that You have put me in this time and this place to sparkle and show how great You are. I would like to be a shining jewel so that people realize that You are real and that You are amazing. Please show me how I can do that this week. Amen.

Knit Together

"This is what I have asked of God for you: that you will be encouraged and knit together by strong ties of love."

Colossians 2:2, TLB

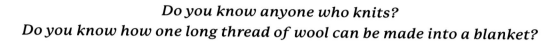

Do you know anyone who knits?
Do you know how one long thread of wool can be made into a blanket?

Have you ever owned a woolen cardigan? A woolen cardigan is knit, stitch by stitch, and the buttons down the front are sewn on by the woolen thread so that each is held in place and does its job as part of the cardigan. On its own, a button is just a button. When it's sewn onto a cardigan, it's part of something bigger and much more special and useful.

Christians have been knit together by God. We are knit together with everyone else in our church by love. Because we all know that Jesus loves us, we want to show that same love to everyone else who is part of our church. That holds us together—each of us in our place as a part of our church. On our own, we're just one person. When we're knit into God's people, we're part of something much bigger and much more special and useful.

Paul, who wrote this verse, also talks about the church as being like a body. Your body was knit together by God as you grew inside your mom (Psalm 139:13). Your body has many parts that do different things, and they come together in your body. The Bible says your church is a body—it has many people who do different things, and they are knit together by God to become part of something special.

A Christian is someone who is knit together with other Christians in a church. Jesus' love for us and our love for each other are what hold us together. And that means we're part of something big and special and useful—just like a button on a woolen cardigan.

 is for Knit Together.

What kinds of different things do people in your church do to serve the rest of the church?

How does it make you feel to be part of something big and special and useful, because God has knit you into His church?

Dear God, thank You for my church and for knitting me into it. Thank You for all the people there who teach me Your word and who show me Your love and who help me praise You. Thank You that it's exciting to be a little part of something much bigger. Please show me how I can love other people in my church. Amen.

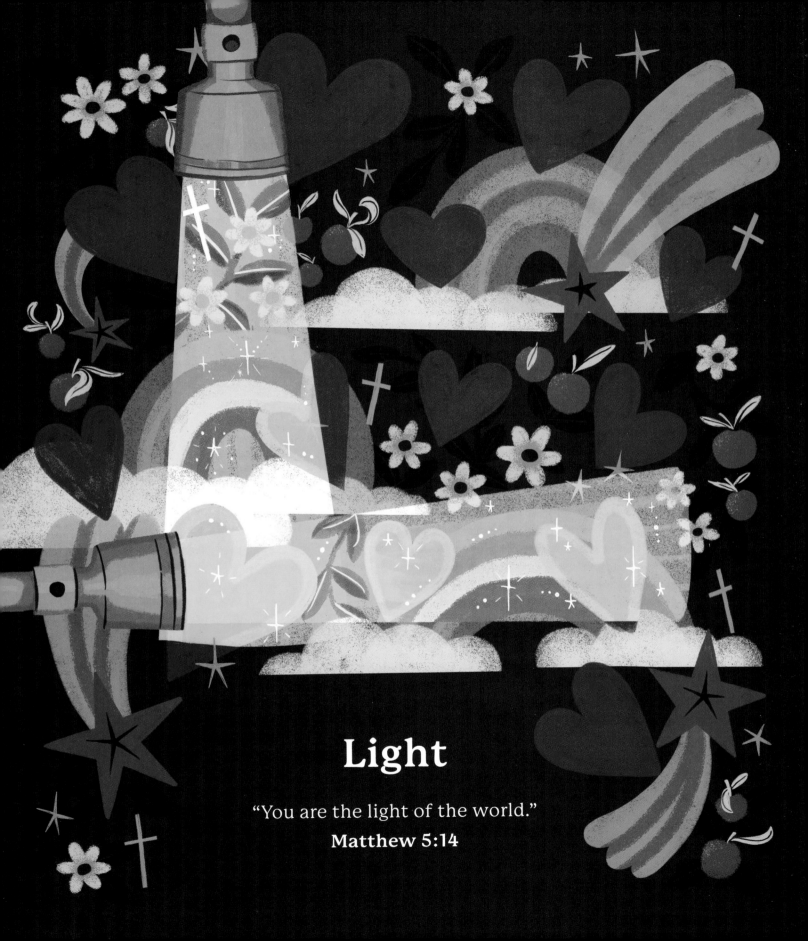

Light

"You are the light of the world."

Matthew 5:14

What do you find difficult to do when it's dark?

Imagine if we had to live in the dark all the time. Without light, we wouldn't be able to see where we needed to get to, and we wouldn't see the way to get there. Without light, we wouldn't be able to see beautiful things around us, and we wouldn't be able to see things that might trip us up and hurt us.

It's much better to live in the light than in the dark.

Jesus says that Christians are like lights in a dark world. If people don't know God, then it's as if they are living in darkness. Because we know the truth about God and about eternity and about how to live in His world, we can show people where they need to get to—heaven—and how to get there—by trusting in Jesus. We can show people how wonderful Jesus is, and we can show people how to live His way—the best way.

We can be the light of the world because Jesus is "the light of the world" (John 8:12). "In him [is] life, and the life [is] the light of men. The light shines in the darkness..." (John 1:4-5). When we trust in Jesus, He gives us life and He shows us how to live. And He gives us the power to shine His light to others. Just as a flashlight needs batteries in order to shine its light, we need Jesus living in us to shine His light through us.

All over the world, Jesus is shining His light through His people. Each of us can share with people the truth about Him and show people that it's great to live His way.

 is for Light.

What does Jesus' "light" give us and show us?

How would you like to ask Jesus to help you shine His light when you are with your friends or at school?

Dear Lord Jesus, thank You that You are the light of the world. Thank You that You came to this world to give people eternal life with You. Thank You that I get to be a way You shine Your light today. Lord Jesus, please help me to show other people what You are like so that they can see that it is great to live with You as their Lord and friend. Amen.

Members

"You are the body of Christ and individually members of it."

1 Corinthians 12:27

***Here is an easy question: how many noses do you have
and where on your body would you find them?***

You have (I hope) only one nose, and you need to know the difference between your nose and your mouth, and the difference between your hands and your feet, and so on.

Imagine if your body was made only out of noses? It would be great at breathing and smelling, but how could you possibly see or speak?!

Our bodies have lots of different parts—and all of them are needed.

Imagine if your feet said, "Because we are not hands, we are not part of this body." Hands are great—you can clap and point and write with them—but without feet, you wouldn't be able to walk!

God has put each bit of your body just where He wanted it to go. He put your nose in the right place so that you can smell with it. He put your nose the right way up so that the rain wouldn't go in your nostrils.

God has done the same in your church. A church is made up of many members—individual people. All of them are different—they are good at different things. All of them are needed—because no one can do everything.

When a boy or girl trusts in Jesus as their Savior and Lord, not only are their sins forgiven and the Holy Spirit comes to live in them, but they are made members of a body, a church. The people in a church belong to each other in the same way that our ears and our nose and our hands and our feet belong to our body.

God has put you in your church to be a member of it—to love and help and share and serve in the way that only you can, and to let others love and help and share and serve you in the way that they can. Every part is in the right place, just as God intends. Including you!

 is for Member.

What would go wrong in church if everyone was good at the one same thing?

What ways can you love and help and share and serve in your church?

Dear God, thank You for making me a member of my church. Thank You that all the people in my church are all different and are all needed. Thank You that I need my church and that my church needs me. Please show me the ways You've given me to love and help and share and serve the other members of my church. Amen.

New Creation

"If anyone is in Christ, he is a new creation."
2 Corinthians 5:17

Have you ever gone shopping for new clothes?

There is a difference between fixing old clothes and buying new ones. If you fix a tear in some old clothes, they are still the same, but just with a new patch. But if you go and buy new clothes, they are totally new. They are completely different!

The Bible says that when someone puts their faith in Christ, they are completely new and totally different. They now belong to His future perfect world—His new creation. They are walking around in this world as a little piece of that future perfect world! A Christian is a new creation.

This means we are completely different, inside and out. It is as though we have thrown our old clothes away and have been given new clothes to wear.

Our old clothes are things like anger, jealousy, and rude talk. These things are to be thrown away! The Bible says that instead of those old clothes, we should "clothe [ourselves] with compassion, kindness, humility, gentleness and patience ... and over all these ... put on love" (Colossians 3:12, 14, NIV).

Every Christian is a new creation. Now we need to wear our new clothes. We show what God's future perfect world is like as we live with kindness, gentleness, patience, and love.

 is for New Creation.

The new creation will be full of kindness, gentleness, patience, and love. How does this make you feel about getting to live there one day?

What would you like God to help you "put on" more and more this week?

Dear God, thank You that one day You will make a perfect new creation for Your people to live in. Thank You that Jesus' followers are already little pieces of that new creation. Until the day you make Your new creation fill this world, please make me able to wear my new-creation clothes, so that I am kind and gentle and patient and loving. Amen.

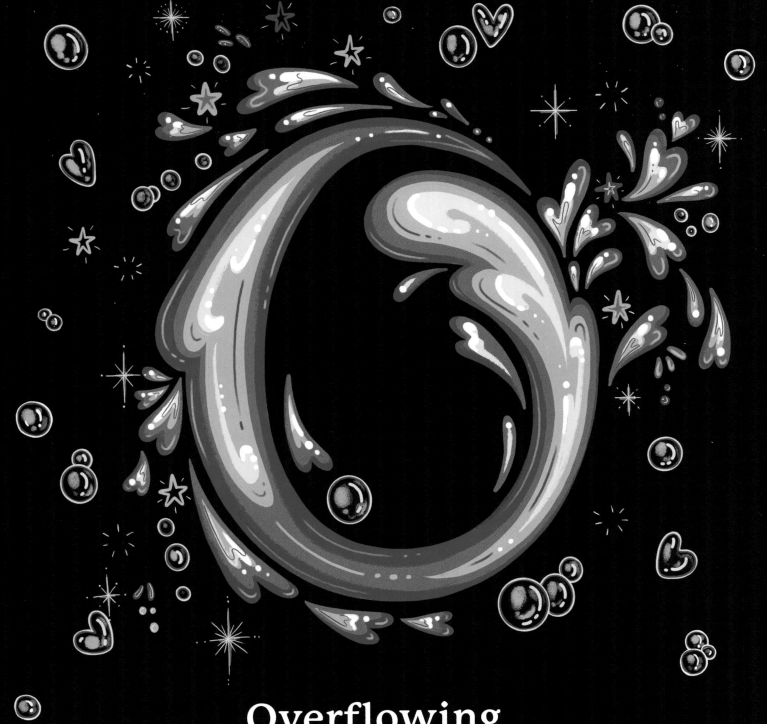

Overflowing

"He who believes in me ... out of his heart will
flow rivers of living water."

John 7:38

How good are you at carrying cups that are very full?

If a cup is full up, then it very easily becomes an overflowing cup! Jesus says that people who believe in Him are full of His Spirit, who lives in their hearts. We are full of His love and truth. And if we're full of these things, then we will overflow with these things. From our hearts will "flow rivers of living water." The love of Jesus and the truth about Jesus will come out of us, in how we live and what we say.

If you bump into someone, you will discover what is inside—what they overflow with. It might be anger or irritation or pride. But the Christian overflows more and more with forgiveness, joy, and peace. Of course, we don't do that perfectly! But we do do that increasingly.

How can you be someone who overflows with love and truth? By filling yourself up with Jesus. You can look at His word, the Bible, to remember how good Jesus is and how great it is to be His friend. You can learn Bible verses to say to yourself during the day. You can enjoy spending time praising Him with His people at your church. You can talk to Him any time, all the time. In all these ways, you can make sure you're filling up with Jesus so that you overflow with His love and His truth.

Next time you're filling up a cup of drink, remember: Jesus wants boys and girls to overflow with His love and truth.

Next time you spill a cup of drink, remember: Jesus wants boys and girls who are like that too!

 is for Overflowing.

What are you going to remember next time you fill a cup or spill a cup?

What Bible verses would you like to memorize so that you can say them to yourself through the day?

> Lord Jesus, thank You that You are love and truth. Thank You that You live in Your people by Your Spirit. Please make me so in love with You and excited about You that Your love and truth overflow from me. Amen.

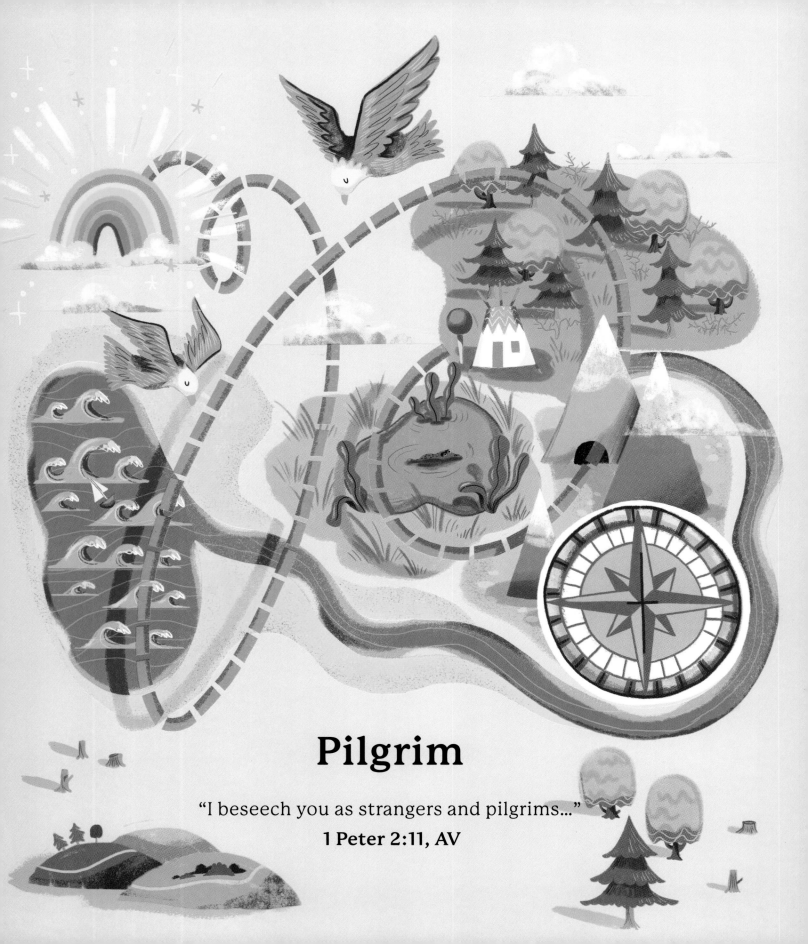

Pilgrim

"I beseech you as strangers and pilgrims…"

1 Peter 2:11, AV

What is the longest journey you have ever been on, and where were you going?
Was the place you were going to worth the effort of getting there?

A "pilgrim" is an old-fashioned word to describe someone who is on a journey, traveling through a land that is not their own, to get to a better place.

Some of the first Europeans to settle in America are known as the "Pilgrim Fathers." In the 1600s, they got on a boat in Britain called the *Mayflower,* and they sailed across the Atlantic Ocean until they reached the land we now call the United States. They were pilgrims who went on a journey, traveling through the sea, to get to what they believed would be a better place.

All Christians are pilgrims. We are on a journey through life. We are traveling through this world, to get to a better place.

Our destination is heaven. We know how to get there because the Bible tells us—it is by trusting Jesus every day until we are there. And we have a guide who can help us along the way—Jesus Himself.

The Christian life is a one-way journey. If you buy a ticket to go somewhere on a bus or a train, a return ticket means that you can go to that place and then come back again. A single ticket takes you there but not back. Christians have a single ticket. We are going to heaven, and we're going to stay in heaven forever!

Everyone has to decide whether to be a pilgrim or a wanderer. A pilgrim is on their way through life to somewhere better. A wanderer is living life without getting anywhere.

If we trust in Jesus, then we are pilgrims. Other people will think Christians are strange because we don't think this world is the most important thing. That's because we know that we are on the way to somewhere much, much better—and so we keep trusting Jesus until the day our journey is over and we are enjoying life with Jesus forever.

is for Pilgrim.

Why is life in heaven better than life right now in this world, do you think?

If we remember we are pilgrims, how will that make a difference when we don't have something in this life that we'd really like?

Dear Lord, thank You that life after death with You in heaven is amazing. Thank You that that is where all Your people are heading. Please keep me trusting in Jesus and traveling as a pilgrim through this world until I get there. Amen.

Qualified

"The Father ... has qualified you to share in the
inheritance of the saints in light."
Colossians 1:12

How tall are you? Are there things you can't do till you are bigger?

In an amusement park, some rides are for anyone, of any age and size. But some rides are bigger and faster, and those rides usually have a sign at the entryway that has a giant measuring ruler on it, showing you how tall you have to be to be allowed on that ride.

If you're tall enough, you qualify for entry. You are allowed down the entryway and onto the ride. If you're not tall enough, you don't qualify. However much you'd like to, you can't go on that ride.

One day God is going to build something for people to enjoy that is much better than an amusement park. He is going to make a perfect world, where nothing goes wrong and everything is always great. It's an "inheritance" for His people—for "the saints."

So, how do you get into that world? How do you qualify for entry?

Some people think you need to be a good person.

Or to go to church every week and read your Bible every day.

Or to do your best to keep God's laws.

But the Bible says that no one can qualify based on who they are or what they do. That's like standing next to a seven-foot ruler in an amusement park and trying to make yourself tall enough! You can't do it.

And that's okay, because God Himself has qualified us. God sent Jesus, His Son, to take our sins and give us His perfection. Jesus has provided all that is necessary for us to qualify for entry. So you don't need to be good enough, or clever or old or tall enough. You just need to say to Jesus, "Lord Jesus, please take my sin and give me Your perfection." And then you can know for sure that you can enter God's forever kingdom.

 is for Qualified.

Why is it great news that God qualifies us for His perfect world, and we don't have to do it ourselves?

Next time you're too small to do something in this world, what would you like to remember about God's forever perfect world?

Dear God, I know that I am not good enough to deserve to be in Your perfect new creation. I am sorry for the wrong things I think, say, and do. Thank You for sending Jesus to take my sin and give me His perfection. Thank You that you have done everything necessary for me to have a place in Your perfect world. Thank you that because of Jesus, I qualify to get in. Amen.

Repenting

"Repent therefore, and turn back, that your
sins may be blotted out."

Acts 3:19

Have you ever changed your mind about something because someone you trust told you that you were wrong?

Sometimes the driver of a car sees a speed-limit sign and realizes they've been driving too fast. They've got their speed wrong. What should they do? They should change their speed, of course! Their mind says, "I have been going at the wrong speed." And so they change their actions.

The Bible's word for what you do when you change your mind about something, and therefore change your actions, is "repent."

Christians are people who trust that Jesus knows best. After all, He is the King that God promised to send. He will rule everywhere for all time. He gets to say what is right and what is wrong. So when we realize that we are doing something that Jesus says we shouldn't do, we repent.

That's how someone becomes a Christian. They realize that they have been living with themselves in charge instead of with Jesus in charge. So they change their mind and they change their actions. They "turn back" to the way they were designed to live, with Jesus as their King. They say, "Jesus, I want You to be in charge of my life."

And when we do this, our sins are "blotted out." Imagine that all the wrong things you have done—all the ways you don't obey Jesus as your King—are written down on a piece of paper. (It would be a big piece, wouldn't it?!) Now imagine God gets a big black marker pen and scribbles all over that piece of paper till you can't see any writing at all. That is what God does with our sin when we repent. He makes it so that it's like it was never there.

But Christians don't just repent once. They keep repenting. That is because every day, there will be ways in which we live with ourselves in charge, instead of Jesus. We think, say, and do things that disobey Jesus. So every day, we repent. We say sorry to Jesus. We thank Jesus for blotting out our sins. And we ask for Him to work in us by His Spirit to enable us to live with Him as our King.

 is for Repenting.

Can you explain what repenting means?

Why is it good to repent every day? Is there anything you'd like to repent of right now?

Dear Father, as we look back over the previous day, here are the things we want to say sorry for... [encourage everyone to say something here]
Thank You that You have blotted out our sins. Please work in us by Your Spirit to enable us to love You as our King and live with You in charge, in the way we think and the things we do. Amen.

Sent

"As the Father has sent me, even so I am sending you."

John 20:21

Have you ever been sent somewhere to give someone a message?
How did you feel about being trusted to do this important job?

God sent His Son into this world to show people His love and tell people how they can live with Him forever.

And God's Son sends His followers into the world to show people His love and tell people how they can live with Him forever.

When Jesus spoke to His disciples, He said that He would send them to be "fishers of men" (Matthew 4:19). Usually, fishers catch fish—and that's the job that a lot of Jesus' first followers had. They wanted to catch fish.

But Jesus had a different job for them to do—a job He gives all His followers. He wanted them to fish for people. That sounds strange! What did He mean?! He meant that He was sending them to speak words about Him that would bring people to see the truth about Him. Just as a fisherman uses a net to bring fish in, Christians are to use their words to bring people to understand who Jesus is.

So Jesus' first followers stopped trying to find fish in the sea to catch, and they were sent out to find people in the world to talk to about Jesus.

You can do that too. You probably talk to lots of people in a week. Some of them won't know who Jesus is. You can show them what Jesus is like by how you treat them. And you can tell them how great Jesus is with your words. Wherever you're going this week, Jesus is sending you there to be a "fisher of men"—to tell people the truth about Him.

 is for Sent.

How do you feel about being sent by Jesus to tell people the truth about Him?

Who would you like to pray for, asking God to give you a chance to talk to them about who Jesus is?

Dear Jesus, thank You for sending me to fish for people by telling them about You. Thank You that I can share the most exciting message ever with people who I meet. Please give me courage to do the job You are sending me to do. Right now, I want to pray that You would give me a chance talk to [answer from second question above] about You. Amen.

Taster

"Taste and see that the LORD is good!"

Psalm 34:8

What is your favorite taste?
How did you find out that you liked it so much?

The only way to find out if something tastes good is to taste it! If someone tells you that strawberries taste good, the only way to know is by putting a strawberry in your mouth and tasting it for yourself. While it is still in your hand, you have no idea whether it will taste yummy or yukky.

It is the same with Jesus. He says that He is the bread of life—that He can give us all we really need in life and give us eternal life (John 6:51). So the Bible tells us to "taste and see that the LORD is good." It is as we "taste" Jesus that we find out how good He is.

Wait, what?! How do you taste a person?! You "taste" Jesus by believing in Him as your Savior and your Lord. As you live with Jesus as your King, you discover that it's good to have Him in charge. As you pray to Jesus when you feel sad, you discover that it's good to have Him to talk to. When we die trusting in Jesus to give us life in heaven, we will discover that it's good to be with him forever.

When we trust Jesus—when we "taste" Him—we discover that He is good: really, really good.

A Christian is someone who believes Jesus. They know Jesus is wonderful because they trust and follow Him. They have "tasted" Him by believing in Him, and they are enjoying Jesus as the best Friend and King they could have. And so every day, they go on tasting Jesus by reading about Him in His Word, the Bible. They love to taste and see how good Jesus is.

 is for Taster.

How and when you do read the Bible? Does it help you love Jesus?

What good things about Jesus would you like to praise Him for now?

Dear Lord Jesus, thank You that knowing You is the best thing ever. Thank You that I can taste how good You are every time I read about You in Your Word. Please keep showing me how great You are, every day. Amen.

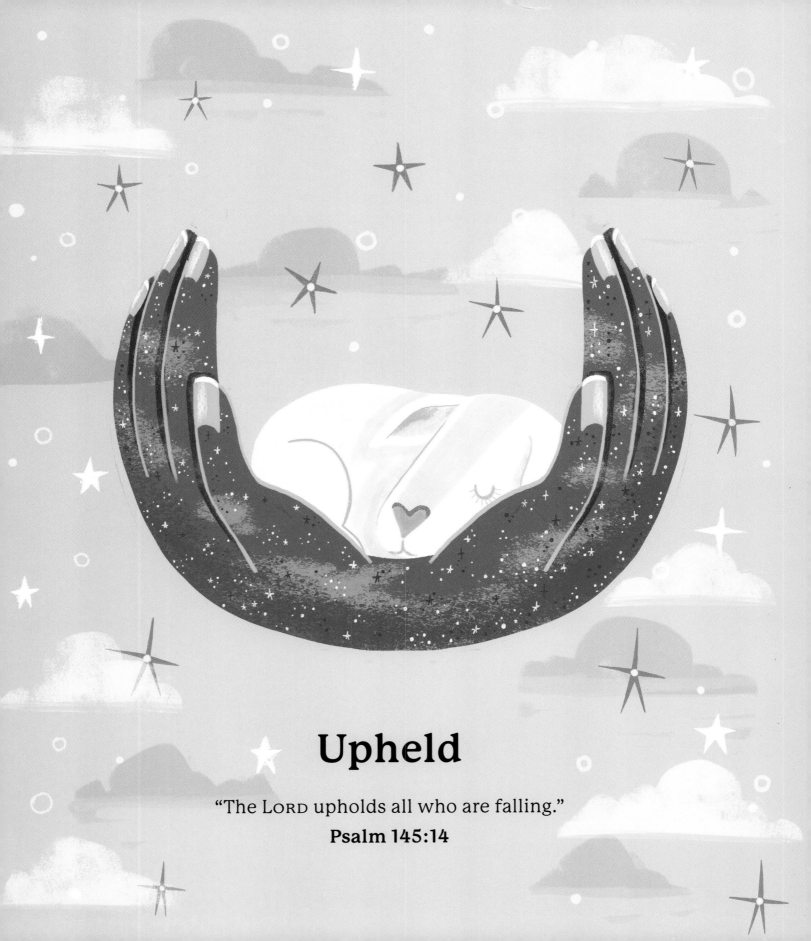

Upheld

"The Lord upholds all who are falling."

Psalm 145:14

Do you know how old you were when you first started walking?
How do you get on with walking at first?

I am guessing that when you were very little and had only just learned to walk, you would sometimes trip. That's why your mom or dad or gran or grandad would walk alongside you.

When you tripped, they were ready. As you were falling, they would catch you. They would stop you bumping your nose or scratching your knees or hurting your hands. You would be held up—or, we could say, you would be upheld. Maybe even now you still need upholding sometimes when you trip.

If somebody is going to uphold you when you fall, they need to be two things.

First, they need to be stronger than you. They need to be able to catch you and hold you and stop you hitting the ground.

Second, they need to be someone who cares for you. They need to want to catch you. They need to be looking out for you.

And if somebody is going to uphold you when you fall, you need one thing.

You need to trust them. You need to have faith that they are strong enough and caring enough to keep their promise to uphold you.

God promises to uphold us when we are falling. When we are worried about something or scared of something, He will help us. When we are unsure what to do, He will guide us. When we are sad, He will comfort us. When we have sinned, He will forgive us.

You can trust God to keep His promise. He is stronger than you, because He is stronger than anything. And He cares for you, because He is the most loving Person of all. So He will uphold you.

 is for Upheld.

If God were strong but not caring, could He uphold you? Why/why not? What about if He were caring but not strong?

When in your own life do you most need to remember that God upholds you as you trust in Him?

> Dear God, thank You that You are stronger than me and stronger than anything. Thank You that You care about me and are more caring than anyone. Thank You that You uphold me. Please give me trust in You to help, guide, comfort, and forgive me. Amen.

Victorious

"This is the victory that has overcome the world—our faith."

1 John 5:4

Have you ever been on the winning team in a sports match?
How did you feel?

Of course, it doesn't really matter if you are victorious or defeated in a soccer match or a baseball game. But the Bible tells us that there are some things in life where it does really matter whether we are victorious. And with those things, we need Jesus to give us the victory.

First, we need Jesus to give us victory over our sin—over the ways we fail to love and obey God. Do you ever get mad, or snatch something that belongs to someone else, or disobey your parents? The Bible says that "the blood of Jesus cleanses us from all sin" (1 John 1:7). Because Jesus died to forgive us, He gives us victory over our sin.

Second, we need Jesus to give us victory over temptation. All of us are tempted to do wrong things, think wrong thoughts, and say wrong words. It is often hard to choose to obey God! Jesus has given His followers His Spirit so that we can say "no" to disobeying God and choose to do what is right. Jesus works in us so that we can have the victory over temptation.

Third, we need Jesus to give us victory over death. After Jesus died, He defeated death by rising back to life and living forever! That's why He is "the resurrection and the life." He promises that "whoever believes in me, though he die, yet shall he live" (John 11:25). We don't need to be scared of dying. It is like falling asleep and then opening our eyes and seeing Jesus. Because Jesus rose from the dead, He gives us victory over death.

Jesus is victorious over sin, over temptation, and over death. If we are on His side, trusting His promises to us, then He shares His victories with us. We are on the winning team.

 is for Victorious.

Why do we need Jesus to give us victory over sin, temptation, and death?

How does it make you feel to know that Jesus has defeated death, so that you can live with Him when you die?

Dear Jesus, thank You that You have won victories for me that I could not win myself. Thank You that You are more powerful than my sin, so that I can be forgiven. Thank You that You are more powerful than any temptation, so I can obey you. Thank You that You are more powerful than death, so I don't need to worry and will live with You forever. Amen.

Worker

"Do your best to present yourself to God as one approved, a worker who has no need to be ashamed."

2 Timothy 2:15

What do you think makes someone a good worker?

God gives all of His people work to do for Him, every day. It might be caring for someone else. It might be saying something kind. It might be teaching someone something about Him from His Word. It might be giving your time to help someone out. It might be using your talents in a church service.

Christians don't work hard so that we can be loved and forgiven by God. No! Christians work because we are already loved and forgiven by God, just by trusting in Jesus.

Christian work is often hard work. And God wants you to "do your best." Some people do the very least that they need to do. They put in as little effort as they can. But other people do the very best they can possibly do. They try as hard as they can. As we live the Christian life, that's how we are to do the work God gives us.

If we do this, then we will have "no need to be ashamed." Imagine a school student doing some work in class. When they have finished, if they have done their best and tried hard, then they can give their work to their teacher with pride. But if they know they have rushed their work and not done it as well as they can, they will hand it in with shame. As we live the Christian life, God wants us to do our work in a way that means we can say, "That's my very best."

That's the kind of worker who is "approved" by God. We work hard so that God will approve of the way we live for Him and obey Him. It's exciting to think that, as you work hard for Him, God will look at you and say, *That's great. I really approve of what you're doing. You're the kind of worker I'm looking for*!

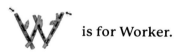 **is for Worker.**

What good works does God give you to do each day?

Do you think you will work harder if you remember that God is watching and approves of your hard work? Why?

Dear God, thank You that You love me not because I work hard but because I trust Jesus. Thank You that You do give me good works to do for You. Please help me to work hard and to remember that You are pleased when Your people do their best in the work You've given them. Amen.

X - Loved

"God shows his love for us in that while we were
still sinners, Christ died for us."

Romans 5:8

How can you show someone that you love them?

When a husband is writing to his wife and he wants to show that he loves her, he might finish his message with an "x." And "x" stands for a kiss—it's a way of saying, "I love you."

When you want to show your parents that you love them, you might give them a real "x"—a real kiss. It's a way of showing "I love you."

We show we love someone by what we do for them—like giving them a kiss.

Have you ever wondered how much God loves you?

Well, he has shown us.

God showed us how much he loves us when Jesus came and died on a cross.

Jesus loves us so much that He chose to come and give up His life, even though we are sinners and don't deserve anything from Him. He did that because He wanted you to enjoy knowing Him, now and forever. Jesus loves us so much that He chose to do the hardest thing it is possible to do, and He chose to do it for us.

The cross tells us how much God loves us. In fact, the Bible says that "as high as the heavens are above the earth, so great is his steadfast love toward those who fear him" (Psalm 103:11). You can't measure the distance between this earth and the heavens. And you can't measure the amount of love that God has for His people.

The † is like God's big, huuuuuuge "X" to you.

So next time you wonder how much God loves you, think about the cross. If you are trusting Jesus as your Lord and Savior, you can know that God has decided to love you, and nothing and no one can ever stop Him. Whatever you are doing, and whether you are feeling happy or sad, strong or scared, you can know that the God who made the world loves you that much.

 is for Loved.

Why does the cross show that God loves His people more than anyone can measure?

How does it make you feel to know that you are loved by God?

Dear Father, thank You that You love me more than I can understand or measure. Thank You that You love me so much that Jesus died on the cross so that now, if I trust in Him, I can enjoy life with You forever. Today, remind me that You love me this much, so that I can know joy even when bad or sad things happen. Amen.

Yoked

"Take my yoke upon you, and learn from me ...
For my yoke is easy, and my burden is light."

Matthew 11:28-29

*If you were a farmer, how would you get a cow or a horse to go
in the direction you wanted them to?*

When we hear the word "yoke," we likely think of the middle of an egg! But that kind of "yolk" is spelled differently. When Jesus talked about a yoke, what He had in mind was a piece of wood that linked two oxen together, so that they could pull a plow behind them. The yoke kept the oxen going in the same direction. Maybe one ox would be older and steadier, and they would know which way to walk. If the other ox was younger and didn't know how to do its job, being yoked would mean the older one could guide it along. And if the yoke was carefully made, it would fit the oxen well. It wouldn't hurt them—it would rest easily on their necks.

So if you were a young ox in the time when Jesus was alive on earth, you would want to have a well-fitting yoke, and you would want to be yoked to a good ox.

Now that we know what a yoke is for, we can understand what Jesus meant when He said, "Take my yoke upon you, and learn from me ... For my yoke is easy, and my burden is light." He was promising that if someone takes His yoke—that is, if they link themselves to Him and learn from Him how to live—then they will find it an easier way to live. Being yoked to Jesus does not weigh a person down, making life worse. Obeying Jesus is the way we were created to live, and so it is the best way to live.

A Christian knows that Jesus loves them and wants what is best for them. A Christian remembers that Jesus said, "If you love me, you will keep my commandments" (John 14:15). So Christians gladly yoke themselves to Him, obeying what He says.

 is for Yoked.

Do you ever find it hard to let yourself be yoked to Jesus, obeying Him? Why is it hard?

Why is it better to obey Jesus than to decide for ourselves how to live?

Lord Jesus, thank You that You came to show us how to live. Thank You that You love us enough to tell us what is best for us. Please help us to learn to take Your yoke upon us, loving You by keeping Your commandments. When we find it hard to obey You, please remind our hearts that You love us and that Your ways are always best. Amen.

Zealous

"[Our] Savior Jesus Christ ... gave himself for us to ... purify for himself a people for his own possession who are zealous for good works."

Titus 2:13-14

What do you get most excited about?

Lots of children are zealous for ice cream. Lots of children are zealous for playtime with their friends.

Not so many children are zealous for tidying up. And not very many children are zealous for going to bed early.

That's because "zealous" is an old word meaning that you really, really, really like something because you are really, really, really excited about it.

We can be zealous about anything. It might be a good thing (like being kind). It might be a bad thing (like getting more and more toys for yourself).

Here are two things that God calls His people to be zealous about.

Number one: good works. Christians are to really, really, really like doing the things that God asks us to do. Maybe today He will give you the chance to share something, or to obey your parents, or to say something kind to someone. And He wants you to be zealous about doing the good things He has lined up for you to do.

Number two: God. God is amazing! He is powerful and strong and kind and gentle. He keeps all His promises, always. He is keeping the whole world spinning and He still makes sure He listens to you when you speak to Him. He loves you and forgives you and lives with you. He is guiding all that you do each day, every day, until He takes you to be with Him and enjoy perfect life forever. So out of everything you have and everyone you know, it's God whom you can be most excited about. It's right that we love God the most of all. God wants us to be zealous about Him!

 is for Zealous.

If someone asked you to explain what the word "zealous" means, what would you say?

What most excites you about what God is like? How does this help you to be zealous about knowing and loving Him?

Dear God, we praise You for who You are. We would like to tell You that we think You are amazing because You are… [take suggestions here]. Please keep reminding us how great You are, so that we will be excited about knowing You, loving You, and obeying You. Please make us more and more zealous for You and for doing the good things You give us to do. Amen.

The Alphabet

Can you remember what each letter stands for?
Can you remember without looking?!

is for **Adopted**

is for **Branch**

is for **Citizen**

is for **Dwelled-In**

is for **Example**

is for **Forgiven**

is for **Giver**

is for **Helper**

is for **Imitator**

is for **Jewel**

is for **Knitted Together**

is for **Light**

is for **Member**

is for **New Creation**

is for **Overflowing**

is for **Pilgrim**

is for **Qualified**

is for **Repenting**

is for **Sent**

is for **Taster**

is for **Upheld**

is for **Victorious**

is for **Worker**

is for **X - Loved**

is for **Yoked**

is for **Zealous**

If you can remember all these, well done! Now see if you can memorize the Bible verse that goes with each letter...

C is for

Christian

thegoodbook
for children

thegoodbook.com | thegoodbook.co.uk
thegoodbook.com.au | thegoodbook.co.nz